HALLOWEEN
AND DAY OF THE DEAD
TRADITIONS AROUND THE WORLD

BY JOAN AXELROD-CONTRADA · ILLUSTRATED BY ELISA CHAVARRI

The Child's World®
childsworld.com

Published by The Child's World®
1980 Lookout Drive • Mankato, MN 56003-1705
800-599-READ • www.childsworld.com

PHOTOS
Cover: George Rudy/Shutterstock.com
Interior: Tijana Moraca/Shutterstock.com, 5; ruewi/
Shutterstock.com, 9; Robson90/Shutterstock.com, 11;
Benjamin Lopez G/Shutterstock.com, 13; AP Photo/Juan
Karita, 17; Lucy Brown/Shutterstock.com, 21; The Observer
MY/Shutterstock.com, 25; FabrikaSimf/Shutterstock.com, 29;
antoniodiaz/Shutterstock.com, 30

ISBN 9781503850163 (Reinforced Library Binding)
ISBN 9781503851061 (Portable Document Format)
ISBN 9781503851825 (Online Multi-user eBook)
LCCN 2021930127

Printed in the United States of America

ABOUT THE AUTHOR

Joan Axelrod-Contrada is the author of more
than 20 books for children. She's written books
about ghosts and mummies in addition to
Halloween. Joan began her career writing for
newspapers such as the *Boston Globe*. She lives
in Western Massachusetts.

ABOUT THE ILLUSTRATOR

Elisa Chavarri is a Peruvian illustrator who
works from her home in northern Michigan.
She loves to create artwork that inspires
curiosity and happiness in people of all ages.

TABLE OF CONTENTS

CHAPTER ONE   **A SCARY NIGHT** 4

CHAPTER TWO   **HALLOWEEN HISTORY** 6

CHAPTER THREE   **IRELAND: HALLOWEEN** 8

CHAPTER FOUR   **POLAND: ALL SAINTS' DAY,**
ALL SOULS' DAY 10

CHAPTER FIVE   **MEXICO: *DÍA DE LOS MUERTOS*** 12

CHAPTER SIX   **BOLIVIA: DAY OF THE SKULLS** 16

CHAPTER SEVEN   **HAITI: SPIRITS OF THE DEAD** 18

CHAPTER EIGHT   **GUATEMALA: DAY OF THE DEAD**
KITE FLYING 20

CHAPTER NINE   **NIGERIA: FESTIVAL OF SPIRIT DANCERS** . . .22

CHAPTER TEN   **CHINA: HUNGRY GHOST FESTIVAL** 24

CHAPTER ELEVEN   **JAPAN: FESTIVAL OF THE LANTERNS** 26

UP CLOSE 28

HANDS-ON 30

GLOSSARY 31

LEARN MORE 32

INDEX 32

CHAPTER ONE

A SCARY NIGHT

It is Halloween night. Ghosts and skeletons roam the streets. Of course, they're not real ghosts and skeletons. They're just people in **costumes**. Will you dress up for Halloween this year? Will you choose a scary costume or a fun one?

Many children in the United States go trick-or-treating on Halloween. They walk door to door. They ring the doorbell and say, "Trick or treat!" People at each house give them candy. People carve faces in pumpkins. These are jack-o'-lanterns. Some people **decorate** their houses. They might put up lights, fake spider webs, or other scary decorations.

Festivals of the dead such as Halloween happen around the world. In the United States, Halloween **celebrates** all scary things. Other festivals of the dead are for remembering lost loved ones. Many festivals mix these ideas. Candles glow and pictures of skeletons decorate windows. In many countries, families offer gifts of food and flowers to the dead.

Children in the United States go trick-or-treating on Halloween.

CHAPTER TWO

HALLOWEEN HISTORY

Halloween is a night for scary things. It has roots in very old holidays for the dead. The Celtic people lived in the British Isles thousands of years ago. They celebrated their own scary holiday on October 31. They called it *Samhain* (SOW-in). This means "summer's end." Winter began on November 1. It was cold and dark. Food might run out. The smell of dead leaves filled the air. People thought about the dead.

The Celts believed the souls of the dead came back to earth on October 31. Some of these spirits could be mean and angry. Villagers wore masks to trick them.

The Christian religion came to the British Isles many years later. Some new beliefs mixed with old beliefs. Christians celebrated All Saints' Day, also called All Hallows Day, on November 1. They had All Souls' Day on November 2nd. All Hallows Eve became Halloween for short. In England, people went "a-souling" door to door. They asked for sweet buns called soul cakes.

CHAPTER THREE

IRELAND: HALLOWEEN

People in Ireland have dressed in scary costumes for thousands of years. Today the Irish celebrate Halloween as Americans do. Stores sell Halloween costumes, decorations, and treats. Before Halloween, families listen to scary stories. People put on costumes on Halloween. They go trick-or-treating.

After trick-or-treating, they light big fires or go to parties. They eat *barmbrack* (BARM-brak), a special Halloween fruitcake. Baked inside the barmbrack are small items that tell fortunes. A ring means the person will be getting married soon. The Irish used to carve turnips. Now they carve pumpkins into jack-o'-lanterns.

People carve pumpkins into jack-o'-lanterns.

CHAPTER FOUR

POLAND: ALL SAINTS' DAY, ALL SOULS' DAY

People in Poland remember lost loved ones on November 1 and November 2. These are All Saints' Day and All Souls' Day. Polish people celebrate the dead in church. They also tell tales of ghosts and wandering souls.

People set places at the table for the spirits of the dead. Hosts serve old-fashioned foods to make the dead feel at home. They bake a special bread called *zaduszki* (zah-DOOSH-key). The long loaves look like wrapped-up bodies. Zaduszki also means "All Souls' Day."

Relatives travel from far away to visit the graves of their loved ones. They stay overnight and bring gifts for the children. Everyone goes to the graveyard at night. Family members clean tombstones. They bring flowers, pray, and light candles for the dead. People write down the names of their lost loved ones. They write on special sheets of paper called *wypominki* (vih-poh-MEEN-kee). On All Souls' Day, the priest reads off the names in church.

Polish graveyards are filled with candles on All Souls' Day.

CHAPTER FIVE

MEXICO: *DÍA DE LOS MUERTOS*

Bright yellow flowers are everywhere on the *Día de los Muertos* (DEE-ah day lohs MWAIR-tohs) in Mexico. This is the Day of the Dead. Mexicans celebrate every year from October 31 to November 2. This is a Christian holiday. But native Mexican **traditions** are still part of the celebration. These are hundreds of years old.

People call the marigold the flower of the dead. Its petals spread out like rays of the sun. Family members lay down paths of marigolds to guide the spirits home.

Marketplaces are busy. People buy colorful sugar skulls. Bakers sell *pan de muerto* (pahn day MWAIR-toh), the traditional bread of the dead. Skeleton statues called *calaveras* (kah-lah-VEH-rahs) make people smile. These skeletons are dressed up like the living. They show the hobbies and jobs of lost loved ones. One calavera plays the drums. Another drives a truck. Yet another sells ice cream.

People in Mexico decorate with yellow marigolds and colorful skulls to celebrate the Day of the Dead.

Families build **altars** for the dead. These are called *ofrendas* (oh-FREN-dahs). Most ofrendas rest on tabletops. Each soul gets its own candle. Relatives place photos of their loved ones on the altars. They set out some of their favorite things.

People eat special food on October 31. *Mole* (MOH-lay) is a sauce spiced with chocolate and cinnamon. Mexicans eat this on chicken. *Tamales* (tah-MAH-lays) are corn dumplings stuffed with meat and chili. Each tamale is wrapped in corn leaves. After dinner, there are fun activities. Masked actors perform at night. Trick-or-treaters visit houses.

Family members gather at the graveyards on the night of November 1. They decorate the graves. They light candles for the dead. People sell food on the streets. Strolling musicians play songs. Some people stay in the graveyard all night long.

CHAPTER SIX

BOLIVIA: DAY OF THE SKULLS

Many Bolivians celebrate the Day of the Skulls. It is on November 9. People decorate the skulls of dead bodies. They put flowers and hats on the skulls, too. They believe the skulls bring good luck. They believe the skulls protect them from evil and even work magic.

The holiday started with the Aymara people. These people are native to Bolivia. They call the skulls *natita* (nah-TEE-tah). This means "flat noses." The Aymara hold their natitas in bundles like babies. Some skulls belong to family members. Others come from strangers buried in unnamed graves. The owners give the skulls new names.

On the Day of the Skulls, thousands gather at the main graveyard in La Paz. La Paz is the capital of Bolivia. The people sing and dance. They offer bread, flowers, and sweets to the skulls. Some people ask the skulls for favors. At the end of the day, the Aymara lay their natitas back on their altars.

People carry their natitas to church to be blessed during the Day of the Skulls in La Paz, Bolivia.

CHAPTER SEVEN

HAITI: SPIRITS OF THE DEAD

All Souls' Day in Haiti is November 2. The people dress up in purple, white, and black. Those are the colors of the *Vodou* (VOH-doo) spirits of the dead.

The Vodou religion mixes many traditions. Slave traders brought Africans to Haiti hundreds of years ago. The Africans had their own religions. Today most Haitians are Christian. Vodou mixes African and Christian beliefs.

In Vodou, the spirits of the **underworld** are *Ghedes* (GAY-days). Their leader is Baron *Samedi* (SAH-muh-dee). The colorful spirit wears a top hat and carries a cane.

The Festival of Ghede is on All Souls' Day. People wear their best clothes for church. Then they change into costumes for the festival. They dust their faces with white flour. They bring offerings to Samedi. Drums pound and dancers whirl. Some people splash vinegar on their bodies. They believe it protects them from evil.

CHAPTER EIGHT

GUATEMALA: DAY OF THE DEAD KITE FLYING

Guatemalans celebrate the Day of the Dead on November 1. They fly colorful kites over graveyards. Some people believe the kites can reach spirits in heaven.

Santiago *Sacatepéquez* (sah-kah-tay-PAY-qwez) is a small town in Guatemala. People there start planning their kite festival 40 days ahead of time. Men cut bamboo, a woody plant, for the frames of the kites. They use colored tissue paper to make the kites. They use hundreds of sheets of paper. Some kites are 40 feet (12 m) long. That's as big as seven people!

Families throughout Guatemala share a dish called *fiambre* (FYAM-bray). This means "served cold." Fiambre has up to 50 ingredients. It has vegetables soaked in vinegar. Meats such as ham and sausage add flavor. Some families spend days making a special fiambre.

In Santiago Sacatepéquez, people make large brightly colored kites for the Day of the Dead.

CHAPTER NINE

NIGERIA: FESTIVAL OF SPIRIT DANCERS

Nigerians celebrate the Festival of the Spirit Dancers. Leaders set the festival dates. The dates change every year. The festival starts with beating drums. People call out the names of the dead.

Masked men called *Egungun* (eh-GOON-goon) pretend to be the ancestors. They wear layers of cloth from head to toe. The Egungun dress as spirits in their costumes. Some Egungun dress up as animals. They slither like snakes and pounce like leopards. They carry magic medicines.

The dancers make their voices sound different. No one can tell who they are. They visit the graves and homes of the dead. Then they dance through town and bless the crowd.

CHAPTER TEN

CHINA: HUNGRY GHOST FESTIVAL

People celebrate the Hungry Ghost Festival in China in August. This is the month of the seventh moon in China. The festival begins with Buddhist priests performing **ceremonies**. These ceremonies open the gates of the underworld. The hungry ghosts are free to roam.

Families set out pink dumplings for the hungry ghosts. People burn pretend money, houses, cars, and other valuable things. The burned things are for the souls in the underworld. Halfway through the month, priests toss out rolls and candies. Children rush in for the treats.

Angry ghosts are said to stay by the water. Some people stay indoors to avoid them. They're afraid the ghosts might steal their bodies. The Hungry Ghost Festival ends when the priests close the gates of the underworld. The ghosts are thought to scream when they leave.

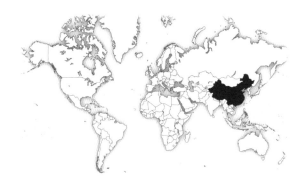

A young boy lights incense sticks
during the Hungry Ghost Festival.

CHAPTER ELEVEN

JAPAN: FESTIVAL OF THE LANTERNS

Families in Japan celebrate *Obon* (oh-BOHN). Obon is also called the festival of **lanterns**. The festival lasts three days in August. People hang lanterns outside their homes. The lanterns glow like full moons. They welcome back the dead. People clear weeds from hillsides and mountaintops. They clear a path for the spirits. Dragonflies flutter down. They are thought to bring the spirits of the dead.

Food, music, and dancing honor the ancestors. People perform folk dances in a circle. They are called *Bon Odori* (bohn oh-DOH-ree), or "dance of Obon." Many female dancers wear silk kimonos. These are long, beautiful dresses with wide sleeves. Often women carry fans or flowers in their hands.

On the last day of the festival, families make little paper boats. They put a candle in each boat. They float the boats down the rivers and bays of Japan. The boats send the spirits back to the land of the dead.

UP CLOSE

A Halloween Song from England

Trick-or-treating can be traced back to the old English custom of going door to door "a-souling" for soul cakes.

Soul Cake (Souling Song)
Chorus:
A soul! a soul! a soul cake!
Please, good Missus, a soul cake!
An apple, a pear, a plum, or a cherry,
Any good thing to make us all merry,
One for Peter, two for Paul,
Three for Him who made us all.

Verse 1:
God bless the master of this house,
The mistress also,
And all the little children
That round your table grow.
Likewise young men and maidens,
Your cattle and your store;
And all that dwells within your gates,
We wish you ten times more.

(*Chorus*)
Verse 2:
Down into the cellar,
And see what you can find,
If the barrels are not empty,
We hope you will prove kind,
With your apples and strong beer,
And we'll come no more a-souling
Till this time next year.

(*Chorus*)
Verse 3:
The lanes are very dirty,
My shoes are very thin,
I've got a little pocket
To put a penny in.
If you haven't got a penny
a ha'penny will do;
If you haven't got a ha'penny,
It's God bless you!

HANDS-ON

Mexican Bread of the Dead

Make your own Mexican bread of the dead. What you need:

Ingredients

- 1 pound (454 g) pizza dough or sweet bread dough
- flour
- confectioners' sugar
- cooking spray (or other baking grease)

Directions

1. Preheat oven to 350 degrees Fahrenheit (177°C). A grown-up should do this step.
2. Divide dough into one large 3-inch (8 cm) ball and one small 2-inch (5.1 cm) ball, using flour for easy handling.
3. Flatten large ball into a 5-inch (13 cm) round base.
4. Shape dough from small ball into a skull and crossbones and put on base.
5. Bake on a greased cookie sheet for 35 minutes. A grown-up should put the bread in the oven and take it out when it is done.
6. Dust with confectioners' sugar.
7. Enjoy!

GLOSSARY

altars (ALL-turz) Altars are tables or stands used in religious rituals. Some people set up altars to honor their lost loved ones.

celebrates (SEL-uh-brayts) When someone celebrates something, he or she observes or take notice of something in a special way. Halloween celebrates scary things.

ceremonies (SAYR-uh-moh-nees) Ceremonies are events that are organized to celebrate special things. There are many ceremonies on the Day of the Dead.

costumes (KAHS-tooms) Costumes are clothes worn to change people's looks. We wear costumes on Halloween.

decorate (DEK-uh-rayt) To decorate is to make something look prettier, more colorful, or better in some way. We want to decorate our house for Halloween.

hallows (HAL-ohs) Hallows are things that are holy. People celebrate All Hallows Day.

lanterns (LAN-turns) Lanterns are small decorative lights. People hang lanterns during the Japanese holiday Obon.

traditions (truh-DISH-uns) Traditions are ways of thinking or acting communicated through culture. Many cultures have traditions for honoring the dead.

underworld (UHN-der-wurld) The underworld is the land of the dead believed to be under the earth in some cultures. Some people believe spirits come back from the underworld.

LEARN MORE

Books

Heinrichs, Ann. *Celebrating Halloween.*
Mankato, MN: The Child's World, 2022.

Shofner, Melissa Raé. *The Story Behind Halloween.*
New York, NY: PowerKids Press, 2020.

Websites

Visit our website for links about Halloween and Day of the
Dead traditions around the world: childsworld.com/links

*Note to Parents, Teachers, and Librarians: We routinely verify our Web links to make sure
they are safe and active sites. So encourage your readers to check them out!*

INDEX

ancestors, 4, 6, 10, 12, 15, 22, 26

candles, 4, 10, 15, 26

costumes, 4, 8, 18, 22

dancing, 16, 18, 22, 26

decorations, 4, 8, 15, 16

flowers, 4, 10, 12, 16, 26

ghosts, 4, 10, 24

gifts, 4, 10

graveyards, 10, 15, 16, 20, 22

masks, 6, 15, 22

pumpkins, 4, 8

religion, 6, 12, 18, 24

skeletons, 4, 12

skulls, 12, 16

treats, 4, 6, 8, 16, 24

trick-or-treating, 4, 5, 8, 15